The Reading Woman II

M000187743

Pomegranate

SAN FRANCISCO

Pomegranate Communications, Inc.
19018 NE Portal Way, Portland OR 97230
800 227 1428; www.pomegranate.com

Pomegranate Europe Ltd.
Unit 1, Heathcote Business Centre, Hurlbutt Road
Warwick, Warwickshire CV34 6TD, UK
[+44] 0 1926 430111; sales@pomeurope.co.uk

ISBN 978-0-7649-4109-2
Pomegranate Catalog No. AA398

Conceived by Maxine Rose Schur

Pomegranate publishes books of postcards on a wide range of subjects.
Please contact the publisher for more information.

Cover designed by Patrice Morris
Printed in Korea
25 24 23 22 21 20 19 18 17 16   12 11 10 9 8 7 6 5 4 3

To facilitate detachment of the postcards from this book, fold each card along its perforation line before tearing.

A book is like a garden carried in the pocket.
—Arab proverb

Whether routes to escape or paths to enlightenment, books create enticing worlds so absorbing to the reader that other realities fade away. A painting of a woman immersed in a book suggests a story of its own: the woman is at peace, or not; perhaps she is silently thrilled by the words she reads. Is she stealing a moment from daily routine to indulge her love of literature? Is she studiously searching the pages for illumination? Is this book the one that will change her life?

Little wonder that the reading woman has appeared in art for hundreds of years. She is a beautiful enigma, an untold tale, a fragment of a life momentarily set free from its long, complex story.

This book of postcards presents thirty quietly joyous studies of women at their books or letters. All are from the collection of the Museum of Fine Arts, Boston.

The Reading Woman II

Micah Williams (American, 1782–1837)
Portrait of a Lady, about 1820
Pastel, 62.9 x 52.1 cm (24¾ x 20½ in.)
Museum of Fine Arts, Boston
Gift of Maxim Karolik for the M. and M. Karolik Collection
of American Watercolors and Drawings, 1800–1875, 60.1105

BOX 808022   PETALUMA   CA 94975

Pomegranate

The Reading Woman II

Laura Coombs Hills (American, 1859–1952)
Fire Opal (Grace Mutell), 1899
Watercolor on ivory, 15.2 x 12.1 cm (6 x 4¾ in.)
Museum of Fine Arts, Boston
Gift of Laura Coombs Hills, 51.1926

Pomegranate

BOX 808022   PETALUMA   CA 94975

The Reading Woman II

Childe Hassam (American, 1859–1935)
Lady Reading, 1898
Watercolor, 48.6 x 30.8 cm (19⅛ x 12⅛ in.)
Museum of Fine Arts, Boston
Bequest of Kathleen Rothe, 65.1303

BOX 808022   PETALUMA   CA 94975

Pomegranate

The Reading Woman II

Edmund Charles Tarbell (American, 1862–1938)
Girl Reading, 1909
Oil on canvas, 81.9 x 72.4 cm (32¼ x 28½ in.)
Museum of Fine Arts, Boston
The Hayden Collection—Charles Henry Hayden Fund, 09.209

BOX 808022   PETALUMA   CA 94975

Pomegranate

The Reading Woman II

Unidentified artist (American, mid-nineteenth century)
Girl with a Gray Cat, about 1840
Oil on canvas, 113.4 x 88.9 cm (44⅝ x 35 in.)
Museum of Fine Arts, Boston
Gift of Martha C. Karolik for the M. and M. Karolik
Collection of American Paintings, 1815–1865, 47.1251

BOX 808022   PETALUMA   CA 94975

Pomegranate

The Reading Woman II

Kitagawa Utamaro II (Japanese, dates unknown)
Young Woman Reading a Letter
Edo period, c. latter half of the Bunka era (1810–1818)
Hanging scroll; ink and color on silk
Image: 105.7 x 32.4 cm (41⁵⁄₈ x 12¾ in.)
Museum of Fine Arts, Boston
William Sturgis Bigelow Collection, 11.7929

BOX 808022   PETALUMA   CA 94975

Pomegranate

The Reading Woman II

James Abbott McNeill Whistler (American, active in England, 1834–1903)
Reading by Lamplight, 1858
Etching and drypoint, printed in brown ink, 31.9 x 20.1 cm
(12⁹/₁₆ x 7¹⁵/₁₆ in.)
Museum of Fine Arts, Boston
Gift of Melinda and James Rabb, 1999.359

BOX 808022   PETALUMA   CA 94975

Pomegranate

The Reading Woman II

Erastus Salisbury Field (American, 1805–1900)
Margaret Gilmore, about 1845
Oil on canvas, 137.5 x 86.7 cm (54⅛ x 34⅛ in.)
Museum of Fine Arts, Boston
Bequest of Maxim Karolik, 64.451

BOX 808022   PETALUMA   CA 94975

Pomegranate

The Reading Woman II

Edward Wilbur Dean Hamilton (American, 1864–1943)
Summer at Campobello, New Brunswick, about 1900
Oil on canvas mounted on Masonite, 71.1 x 71.1 cm (28 x 28 in.)
Museum of Fine Arts, Boston
Bequest of Maxim Karolik, 64.463

BOX 808022 PETALUMA CA 94975

Pomegranate

The Reading Woman II

Edgar Degas (French, 1834–1917)
Visit to a Museum, about 1879–1890
Oil on canvas, 91.8 x 68 cm (36⅛ x 26¾ in.)
Museum of Fine Arts, Boston
Gift of Mr. and Mrs. John McAndrew, 69.49

BOX 808022   PETALUMA   CA 94975

Pomegranate

The Reading Woman II

Kondō Katsunobu (Japanese, active about 1716–1736)
Courtesan Reading a Book
Edo period, Kyōhō era (1716–1736)
Hanging scroll; ink and color on paper
Image: 48.9 x 61.7 cm (19¼ x 24⁵/₁₆ in.)
Museum of Fine Arts, Boston
William Sturgis Bigelow Collection, 11.7504

BOX 808022   PETALUMA   CA 94975

Pomegranate

The Reading Woman II

George Romney (English, 1734–1802)
Portrait of Two Girls (Misses Cumberland), about 1772–1773
Oil on canvas, 73.7 x 63.5 cm (29 x 25 in.)
Museum of Fine Arts, Boston
Robert Dawson Evans Collection, 17.3259

BOX 808022   PETALUMA   CA 94975

Pomegranate

The Reading Woman II

Migita Toshihide (Japanese, 1863–1925)
Woman Reading a Letter
Publisher: Kokkeidō
Late Meiji era
Relief print; ink and metallic pigment on card stock
8.8 x 13.8 cm (3⁷/₁₆ x 5⁷/₁₆ in.)
Museum of Fine Arts, Boston
Leonard A. Lauder Collection of Japanese Postcards, 2002.2436

BOX 808022   PETALUMA   CA 94975

Pomegranate

The Reading Woman II

Mary S. Chapin (American, nineteenth century)
Solitude, 1815–1820
Watercolor over graphite pencil on paper, 38.7 x 34.6 cm
(15¼ x 13⅝ in.)
Museum of Fine Arts, Boston
Gift of Maxim Karolik for the M. and M. Karolik Collection
of American Watercolors and Drawings, 1800–1875, 60.469

BOX 808022   PETALUMA   CA 94975

Pomegranate

The Reading Woman II

Auguste Toulmouche (French, 1829–1890)
Reading Lesson, 1865
Oil on canvas, 36.5 x 27.6 cm (14³/₈ x 10⁷/₈ in.)
Museum of Fine Arts, Boston
Gift of Francis A. Foster, 24.1

BOX 808022   PETALUMA   CA 94975

Pomegranate

The Reading Woman II

Winslow Homer (American, 1836–1910)
Two Girls Looking at a Book, about 1877
Watercolor on paper, 13.6 x 22 cm (5⅜ x 8¹¹/₁₆ in.)
Museum of Fine Arts, Boston
Bequest of Katharine Dexter McCormick, 68.572

BOX 808022 PETALUMA CA 94975

Pomegranate

The Reading Woman II

Mary Stevenson Cassatt (American, 1844–1926)
Mrs. Duffee Seated on a Striped Sofa, Reading, 1876
Oil on panel, 34.3 x 26.7 cm (13½ x 10½ in.)
Museum of Fine Arts, Boston
Bequest of John T. Spaulding, 48.523

BOX 808022   PETALUMA   CA 94975

Pomegranate

The Reading Woman II

Frank Duveneck (American, 1848–1919)
A Girl Reading, 1877
Oil on panel, 61 x 51.1 cm (24 x 20⅛ in.)
Museum of Fine Arts, Boston
The Hayden Collection—Charles Henry Hayden Fund, 23.119

BOX 808022   PETALUMA   CA 94975

Pomegranate

The Reading Woman II

John George Brown (American, b. England, 1831–1913)
Reading on the Rocks, Grand Manan, about 1877
Oil on canvas, 58.4 x 38.1 cm (23 x 15 in.)
Museum of Fine Arts, Boston
Gift of Walstein C. Findlay, Jr., in memory of
William Wadsworth Findlay, 61.1294

BOX 808022 PETALUMA CA 94975

Pomegranate

The Reading Woman II

Yamazaki Joryū (Japanese, active about 1716–1736)
Courtesan Reading a Letter
Edo period, about Kyōhō era (1716–1736)
Panel; ink and color on paper
Image: 35.4 x 51.3 cm (13^{15}/$_{16}$ x 20^{3}/$_{16}$ in.)
Museum of Fine Arts, Boston
Gift of Robert Treat Paine, 61.1227

BOX 808022   PETALUMA   CA 94975

Pomegranate

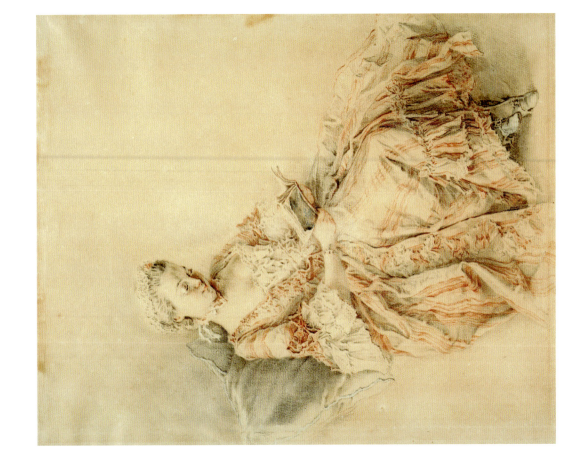

The Reading Woman II

Jacques-André Portail (French, 1695–1759)
Woman Reading, 1735–1759
Black, red, and white chalk with touches of blue watercolor,
46.4 x 36 cm (18¼ x 14³/₁₆ in.)
Museum of Fine Arts, Boston
Bequest of Forsyth Wickes—The Forsyth Wickes Collection,
65.2597

BOX 808022 PETALUMA CA 94975

Pomegranate

The Reading Woman II

John Singer Sargent (American, 1856–1925)
Simplon Pass: Reading, 1911
Transparent and opaque watercolor over graphite,
with wax resist, on paper, 50.8 x 35.6 cm (20 x 14 in.)
Museum of Fine Arts, Boston
The Hayden Collection—Charles Henry Hayden Fund, 12.214

BOX 808022 PETALUMA CA 94975

Pomegranate

The Reading Woman II

William Worcester Churchill (American, 1858–1926)
Leisure, 1910
Oil on canvas, 75.9 x 63.8 cm (29⅞ x 25⅛ in.)
Museum of Fine Arts, Boston
Gift of Gorham Hubbard, 12.325

BOX 808022　PETALUMA　CA 94975

Pomegranate

The Reading Woman II

Torii Kiyonobu I (Japanese, 1664–1729)
Woman Reading a Book
Edo period, early Kyōhō era (1716–1736)
Hanging scroll; ink and color on silk, 37.3 x 50.8 cm (14^{11}/$_{16}$ x 20 in.)
Museum of Fine Arts, Boston
William Sturgis Bigelow Collection, 11.7536

BOX 808022   PETALUMA   CA 94975

Pomegranate

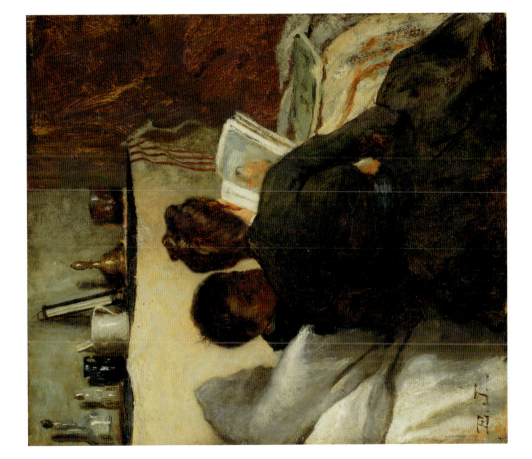

The Reading Woman II

Eastman Johnson (American, 1824–1906)
The Little Convalescent, about 1873–1879
Oil on paperboard, 32.4 x 27.9 cm (12¾ x 11 in.)
Museum of Fine Arts, Boston
Frederick Brown Fund, 40.90

BOX 808022 PETALUMA CA 94975

Pomegranate

The Reading Woman II

Lilian Westcott Hale (American, 1880–1963)
L'Edition de Luxe, 1910
Oil on canvas, 58.4 x 38.4 cm (23 x 15⅛ in.)
Museum of Fine Arts, Boston
Gift of Miss Mary C. Wheelwright, 35.1487

BOX 808022   PETALUMA   CA 94975

Pomegranate

The Reading Woman II

William Morris Hunt (American, 1824–1879)
Girl Reading, 1853
Oil on canvas, 54.6 x 40.6 cm (21½ x 16 in.)
Museum of Fine Arts, Boston
Gift of Mrs. Charles W. Dabney, 93.1455

Pomegranate

BOX 808022   PETALUMA   CA 94975

The Reading Woman II

Henry Bacon (American, 1839–1912)
On the Open Sea—The Transatlantic Steamship "Péreire," 1877
Oil on canvas, 50.2 x 74 cm (19¾ x 29⅛ in.)
Museum of Fine Arts, Boston
Gift of Mrs. Edward Livingston Davis, 13.1692

BOX 808022   PETALUMA   CA 94975

Pomegranate

The Reading Woman II

Ignaz Marcel Gaugengigl (American, b. Germany, 1855–1932)
The Visitor, about 1925
Oil on canvas, 76.2 x 63.5 cm (30 x 25 in.)
Museum of Fine Arts, Boston
Gift of Frederick L. Jack, 35.1223

BOX 808022   PETALUMA   CA 94975

Pomegranate

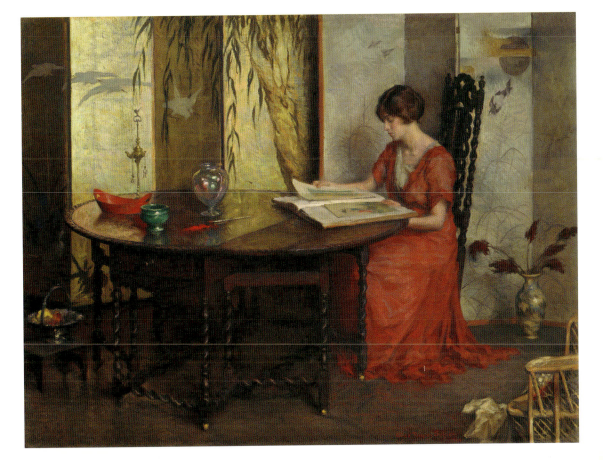

The Reading Woman II

Alice Ruggles Sohier (American, 1880–1969)
Girl in Red, 1926
Oil on canvas, 76.5 x 101.9 cm (30⅛ x 40⅑ in.)
Museum of Fine Arts, Boston
Gift of the Estate of Elizabeth B. Brewster, 2004.255

BOX 808022   PETALUMA   CA 94975

Pomegranate